Always a New Beginning

A GUIDE TO NAVIGATE THE INEVITABLE LOSSES
NOT AS A SHRINKING OF THE OPTIONS
BUT A HOPEFUL ANTICIPATION
OF THE NEW WAYS THAT MAY YET EMERGE.

STEPHEN McCUTCHAN

PRIMIX
PUBLISHING
THE WRITE CHOICE

Primix Publishing
11620 Wilshire Blvd
Suite 900, West Wilshire Center, Los Angeles, CA, 90025
www.primixpublishing.com
Phone: 1-800-538-5788

Published by Primix Publishing: 03/28/2024

ISBN: 979-8-89194-110-6(sc)
ISBN: 979-8-89194-111-3(e)

Library of Congress Control Number: 2024901733

Contents

Always a New Beginning

This booklet offers a spiritual reflection based on the author's experience of moving into the Westminster Shores retirement community in S. Petersburg, Florida. The intention is to provide the reader with some spiritual guidance as they experience the challenge and promise of growing older.

If there is one universal truth, it is that from birth, we are all growing older. For much of our life, we aspire, gain skills, produce, and look forward to the future. Somewhere in our 60's, things begin to change. We become quite conscious of the process of aging. We are not only growing older, but we are also among the elderly. There are lots of products on the market to help us live in denial but our bodies, and occasionally our neighbors, remind us that we are in the last quarter of our life. When we moved to Westminster Shores, most of us recognize that this is the last home in which we will live.

All of our life involves responding to a series of losses. We don't like losses, sometimes we even fear them, but how we choose to respond to them helps shape our experience of loss. Viktor Frankl reminds us in *Man's Search for Meaning* that the last and most precious freedom we have is the freedom to choose how we will respond. Regardless of what is happening to us, we choose how we will respond to that reality. Someone can insult me, and I choose whether to respond with anger, pity, or laughter at the insult and the insulter. How we respond to our losses in life, including the many types of losses we experience in aging, can determine whether we live this season of our life in a healthy or depressive manner.

This booklet intends to help people understand and cope with the losses that accompany our growing older together in the Westminster Shores community. While what we propose finds its foundation in the Abrahamic faith traditions, we believe that what we suggest has a strong psychological foundation as well. We offer it as our gift for the greater good of the whole community of believers and non-believers.

All of the Abrahamic faith traditions share the common understanding that our lives have a divine origin and a divine destination. We believe that the ordinary building blocks of life are signs of God's love and grace. We see signs of that grace in ceremonies such as marriage, funerals, healing, confession, and reconciliation, but they are also present in our physical world: sunsets across the bay, flower petals in the breeze, light-reflecting in the morning dew, lightning in a thunder cloud. People too are conveyors of grace: a child's giggle, a friend's touch, a kind word, a simple hello. In all of these, God reveals God's self, God's presence, and God's desires for us. All of this is grace.

While we do not believe God causes our pain and loss, we do believe God is not absent at such times. God's presence can be experienced in the midst of the pain of loss. Far too often, we do not see, notice, or pay attention, and consequently, we miss the grace. Somehow we must learn how to slow down and pay attention, so we experience the continuing hope, joy, and love in our lives.

There can be great value in remembering. Throughout Scripture, Israel was always recalling what God had done for them in the past as a means of building courage for facing the unknown future. Both in Scripture's recordings of distress and in contemporary therapeutic settings, people are empowered by remembering how they have triumphed in the past. Then they are enabled to reframe their perspective of the future. Recalling past events when we have experienced life-giving moments in the midst of loss can build our trust that it is worth searching for ways to be open to and anticipate new beginnings in the future.

None of this is to minimize the very real hurt and trauma that comes from loss. To tell someone in pain that they should accept this as a blessing in disguise is not helpful. The loss contains real and legitimate pain that needs to be acknowledged and owned.

From the day we are born, we begin to experience loss. Our first loss is when we are pushed out of a warm and cozy womb and into the bright cold world. We come into the world expressing our displeasure and grief in a screeching cry. It would seem that as we age, the losses become more frequent and more profound. They are like little deaths. Parts of ourselves die and will be no more. As older persons, we will never again play shortstop, dance at a prom, or conceive a child. We will not see our dog Midnight or our friend Ed or our father. They all died years ago. Part of moving into the Shores included a decision to live downsized lives. We gave up treasured pieces of furniture or workshops or library collections in order to move here.

As part of this last stage of our lives, losses has become a constant companion. Here at Westminster Shores when we hear the ambulance, we are reminded of the losses of our neighbors and recognize our losses to come. Aging and the experience of loss does not need to be a shrinking of the options but a hopeful anticipation of the new ways and new life that may yet emerge. From a faith perspective, we can learn to recognize the many blessings in our lives, return them to God with thanksgiving, and turn to anticipate different but good gifts in our new stage of life. Building the expectation of grace into our view of life helps prepare us to see our physical death as one more possibility that can be viewed with trust rather than fear.

All of us have experienced much loss, and we all can expect much more loss. We expect finally our own deaths–the loss of our lives here on Earth. Even though in every loss there is a note of grief and sadness that something valuable and precious is gone, every loss contains the seeds of the gift of God's presence and God's love for us. When we are able to anticipate the fulfillment of the promise of such grace amid the loss, we can say with joy and confidence: "ALWAYS A NEW BEGINNING."

Resources for the Community

There are many ways to give ourselves time and space so that we may be more attentive and more aware of the grace permeating our lives.

Some possibilities are:

- Contemplative prayer and meditation
- Spiritual direction
- Slow walks or just sitting quietly
- Conversations with a trusted spiritual advisor or friend
- Walking a labyrinth or meditation trail
- Gardening
- Journaling
- Making use of poetry and music
- Drawing, painting and other arts and crafts

Four Step Process

We offer a four-step process that can help us with our losses. Each of us experiences these steps in different ways. The steps are not necessarily linear. For some, the journey will be a spiral. However, as we go through these steps of healing; our goal is wellness that includes our spiritual, physical, social, emotional, and mental selves.

NAMING OUR PAIN

We are good at deceiving ourselves and others. Someone asks, "how are you doing?" and we routinely answer "I'm fine" even when there is aching deep in our hearts. We deceive ourselves and mask our losses with avoidances of many kinds. When our pet dies, or we have not heard from an old friend in ages, or we can no longer put our pants on without sitting down, each of these is a loss, and until we recognize and deal with them, we are not fine. Naming our losses is a step toward spiritual wellness.

RECOGNIZING GRIEF

Sadness and mourning accompany every loss—even losses that may seem routine or trivial. I don't have room for Mama's sewing machine, I can't play golf anymore, even with hearing aids I don't hear very well—these are losses that cause regret, sadness, and grief. Naming the feelings generated by these losses gives us the freedom to choose how to act on those feelings. Owning our grief is a step toward spiritual wellness.

SAYING IT OUT LOUD

Once we have recognized a loss and the grief that results, we need to say it out loud. We need to speak to another person about both our loss and our pain. Pain tends to isolate us. Speaking it aloud is a step towards rebuilding community. We need to bring it into the light and allow someone we trust with our secrets and confidences to hear it. The other person does not need to say anything, but we make our loss and grief real and something we can work on when we say it aloud. In naming our grief and the feelings that accompany it, we gain freedom to explore how the pain of that grief is affecting our lives so that we have a reason to want to get beyond it. Saying it aloud is a step toward spiritual wellness.

FINDING GRACE

The fourth step is finding the inward grace in our losses. We ask ourselves how God is revealed at work in the midst of our loss. Or if we are a non-believer, we ask is there some goodness that can come out of the loss? The loss is real, and we don't want to deny the pain, but most of us can remember a loss in our lives that resulted in a new beginning. In seeking to be aware of that grace-filled moment, we are not trying to justify the loss but give it meaning that makes the pain more endurable.

Grief might lessen and get easier with time, but it will always be there. Knowing that the grief will always be there makes recognizing the grace in our losses ever more important. Knowing in our hearts the possibility of new beginnings is another step toward spiritual wellness.

An Experiment in Letting Go

First, think of your five senses—taste, smell, touch, hearing, seeing

Choose two you would most hate to lose. Just note them for now.

Now identify 2-3 possible losses that are difficult to adjust to in the following areas:

- Your physical abilities,
- pleasures that you enjoy,
- talents that bring you satisfaction,
- special possessions,
- relationships that are precious.

Notice as you make your choices the resistance that builds in your even considering such losses.

Second, choose one from your list and imagine that you experienced its loss.

- How does that loss affect your sense of self,
- your relationships,
- your pleasure in life,
- what gives your life meaning?

Write two or three sentences exploring that possibility.

Make a note of the emotions evoked as you consider the possibility of such a loss.

You are exploring the imagined sense of grief at this time of loss. What does it mean to let go of that gift in your life?

Third, find a friend and share what you are exploring.

Note how it affects you to share your thoughts and feelings with someone else.

Does it make you feel weaker or stronger as you share your pain?

Does it allow you to gain some perspective and therefore greater control?

Fourth, consider a possible blessing that could be realized from such an experience of loss.

> Note that imagining such a blessing does not justify the loss but only empowers you to think beyond the loss and explore an alternate future.

Each time, as part of the closure with respect to the loss, take a moment to **thank God for the use of that gift** and release it back to God.

> Then, having explored releasing such a gift back to God, open yourself to the possibility of a **new blessing** that might occur as a result of your being willing to move beyond your grief at the loss.

For your first round, you probably chose a loss that while stressful seemed manageable.

> If you want to go deeper, make another choice. Again you will **name** the loss and how it impacts you and identify the feelings of **grief** involved in such an experience.

A New Freedom

There is a sense of freedom that comes from this process. One is given permission to act in new ways, to begin anew. We may experience a chance to grow in our faith, to be transformed in some ways. We are on a healing journey that leads us toward wellness. Grace is a gift we do not control, and where it takes us cannot be foreseen.

And so dear friend we hope that the process we have described will give you the ability to RELINQUISH GRACEFULLY AND ANTICIPATE HOPEFULLY. We can do this by naming our losses and our grief out loud and experiencing the grace in our loss.

WHERE DO WE GO FROM HERE

In addition to providing opportunities for the Westminster Shores' community to read *Always A New Beginning*, we hope you will engage in conversations regarding aging, loss, death, and dying. As a community, we hope to explore a variety of opportunities for people to grieve healthily and to recognize opportunities for renewed joy as they experience a variety of transitions in their lives.

What type of opportunities do you think would be helpful:

- Discussion groups
- Services of wholeness
- Special prayer services
- Developing a labyrinth for personal reflections
- Spiritual Director
- Others

www.ingramcontent.com/pod-product-compliance
Lightning Source LLC
Chambersburg PA
CBHW021006150626
46549CB00012BA/1385